Published by Creative Education
123 South Broad Street, Mankato, Minnesota 56001

Creative Education is an imprint of The Creative Company.
Design by Stephanie Blumenthal
Production design by The Design Lab
Art direction by Rita Marshall

Photographs by Art Resource, NY (Alinari, Erich Lessing, Scala), Corbis (Alinari
Archives, Archivo Iconografico, S.A., Arte & Immagini srl, Bettmann, Historical Picture
Archive, David Lees, Massimo Listri, Araldo de Luca, Michael Nicholson, Reuters,
Royalty-Free, ML Sinibaldi), Getty Images (Hulton Archive, Stock Montage)

Poem from *Michelangelo: His Life, Work and Times* by Linda Murray. © Linda Murray
1984. Reprinted by permission. / Excerpt from Letter, 2 May 1517 by Michelangelo,
from *Michelangelo: Life, Letters and Poetry*, 1987, edited by George Bull, translated by
George Bull & Peter Porter. By permission of Oxford University Press. / Letter from
Michelangelo to Bishop Vigerio or Cardianl Farnese (Tomb of Julius) from
Michelangelo: Life, Letters and Poetry, 1987, edited by George Bull, translated by
George Bull & Peter Porter. By permission of Oxford University Press.

Library of Congress Cataloging-in-Publication Data

Richardson, Adele, 1966–
Michelangelo / by Adele Richardson.
p. cm. — (Xtraordinary artists)
Includes index.
ISBN 1-58341-379-0
1. Michelangelo Buonarroti, 1475–1564—Juvenile literature.
2. Artists—Italy—Biography—Juvenile literature. I. Title. II. Series.

N6923.B9R518 2005
709'.2—dc22   2004063432

First edition

2 4 6 8 9 7 5 3 1

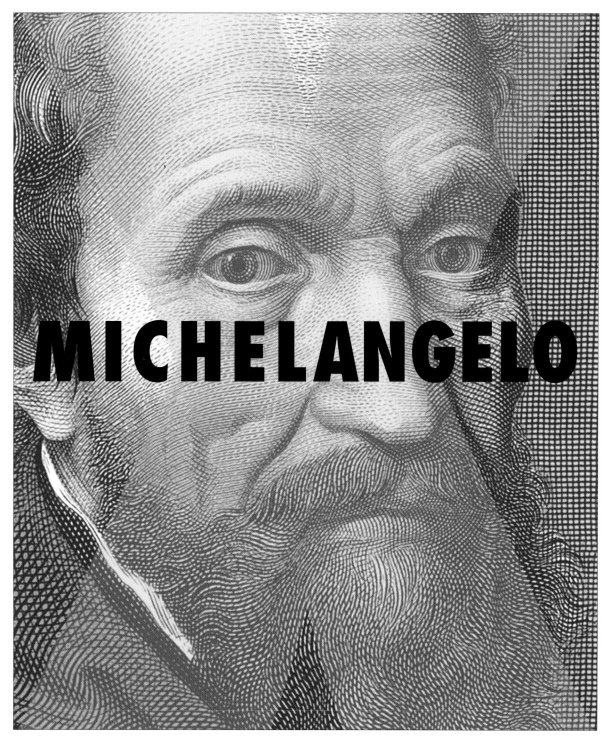

MICHELANGELO

A D E L E   R I C H A R D S O N

CREATIVE 🍎 EDUCATION

Few artists in history have ever achieved his level of expertise. During his lifetime, he was commissioned, and even coerced into employment, by no less than three popes—then the most powerful and influential figures in the world. Today, more than 400 years after his death, his works are revered as sacred and fiercely protected against the ravages of time. His was a life devoted to the creation of monumental and awe-inspiring master-pieces. He cared little for the luxuries that fame could bring, choosing instead to live as a hermit while pursuing his passion until the day he died. Over the centuries, many people have come to believe that Michelangelo was given an extraordinary gift from God—a gift that is still bestowed upon the world today.

Michelangelo di Lodovico Buonarroti Simoni is known to the world simply as Michelangelo. He was born on March 6, 1475, in the small Italian village of Caprese, the second of five sons. Michelangelo's father, Lodovico, was *podesta* of the village. Several months before, Lodovico had traveled the 50 miles (81 km) from Florence with his preg-nant wife, Francesca, and first son, Lionardo, through semi-mountainous terrain to begin his assignment. Lodovico came from an old, respectable family whose fortune and titles of nobility had slowly eroded. He was a proud man who resented his family's loss of sta-tus and would not accept employment he felt was beneath him. As a result, Lodovico was often unemployed. He and Francesca were not wealthy, but they strove to live as genteel a life as possible with what resources they had.

Although he was not born there, Michelangelo considered himself a son of Florence and returned to the city many times throughout his life

From his childhood, Michelangelo became accustomed to the sights and sounds of building construction that surrounded him

The infant Michelangelo was only a few weeks old when the family returned to Florence. Michelangelo, however, did not return with them. Francesca was often ill and could not properly care for her new son. So his parents placed him in the care of a hired wet nurse in Settignano, a village within three miles (4.8 km) of Florence. The wet nurse was both the daughter and wife of stonemasons, whose rhythmic hammering of chisel to stone no doubt lulled the child to sleep. The artist most likely first learned to carve stone during his early years with his foster family. Many years later, Michelangelo would occasionally mention that his love and gift of sculpting surely came to him through his nurse's milk. Michelangelo never knew his mother, who died in 1481 when he was only six years old.

"His body is sinewy and bony rather than fat and fleshy. . . . his body is of medium height, broad across the shoulders [and] his nose is rather squashed. . . . his lips are thin, but the lower one is somewhat thicker . . . his eyes the color of horn, but flecked with sparks of yellow and blue . . . his hair black, as is the beard."

— *Giorgio Vasari, describing Michelangelo's physical appearance*

Sometime between 1482 and 1485, Lodovico enrolled Michelangelo in grammar school to learn reading, writing, and Latin in preparation for life as a gentleman. But Michelangelo cared little for his studies and spent much of his time drawing on scraps of paper. Sometimes he would sneak off with an older boy in the neighborhood named Francesco Granacci. Francesco was an apprentice to the great painter Domenico Ghirlandaio and often brought Michelangelo to the workshop of his master.

Michelangelo's father and uncles were infuriated by the boy's behavior. They believed that being related to an artist—someone who worked with his hands like a com-

mon laborer—would disgrace the family name, and they frequently beat the boy to dissuade him. But Michelangelo would not ignore his talent or abandon his interests. By the time he was 13 years old, he gave up school altogether to focus solely on art.

In early 1488, Michelangelo began an apprenticeship with Domenico Ghirlandaio, who taught him the techniques of fresco painting. As an apprentice, Michelangelo's responsibilities included applying plaster, mixing paints, making brushes, and creating cartoons. To create a cartoon, a master painter's drawing was outlined on a wall. An apprentice or apprentices pricked small holes along the outline and

Lorenzo de Medici's support for artists such as Michelangelo was key to making Florence the center of the Renaissance during the 15th century

filled them with charcoal dust. All the master then had to do was apply the paint. Sometimes apprentices painted portions of a fresco, but only if the areas could not be easily seen.

About one year into his apprenticeship, Michelangelo was introduced to Lorenzo de Medici, the ruler of Florence. Lorenzo, who appreciated great Renaissance art and had an eye for talent, took a liking to Michelangelo and often invited him to his palace. In 1490, 15-year-old Michelangelo moved in with the Medicis and began living and studying alongside Lorenzo's three sons, Piero, Giovanni, and Giulaino. Within the walls of the

palace, Michelangelo was exposed to some of the most powerful and famous people of his time—such as philosopher Marsilio Ficino and poet Angelo Poliziano—and received the cultural education of a nobleman.

Outside the palace, Lorenzo had a private garden filled with sculptures of Greek and Roman figures. He hired master sculptor Bertoldo di Giovanni to attend the garden and its artwork. Historians believe that Bertoldo ran a school of sculpting while at the Medici palace, nourishing Michelangelo's growing love of sculpture for the next two years. In 1492, Lorenzo died, and Michelangelo struck out on his own.

After Michelangelo left the Medici palace, the 17-year-old sought money to send home to his sporadically employed father. His older brother, Lionardo, could not help support the family, as he had become a monk and taken a vow of poverty. Since Michelangelo was the second son, responsibility to become the family's breadwinner fell upon him. It was a burden he would carry for the rest of his life. To earn money, the teenager produced and sold some minor works of art, including a sculpture of the Greek mythological hero Hercules.

Michelangelo was keenly interested in the human body, and his favorite artistic pursuits were nude sculptures in the style of the ancient Greeks and Romans. To gain a

deeper understanding of the human body, Michelangelo spent hours in the Santo Spirito hospital morgue in Rome. Carefully cutting open corpse after corpse, he took special note of how the bodies' veins, muscles, and tendons fit together. Although Michelangelo did not particularly enjoy the macabre work, it gave him the knowledge he needed to create breathtakingly realistic works of art.

After Lorenzo de Medici's death, his son Piero came into power. Piero was not the ruler his father was, however, becoming known for his arrogance and poor military decisions. In 1494, Piero offered to help French king Charles VII invade the city of Naples, but Charles threatened Florence with invasion as well. Rumors of a revolution spread throughout Florence, and in an attempt to save his life, Piero fled the city. Michelangelo grew

More than 50 charcoal drawings by Michelangelo were discovered on the walls of the Medici Chapel in Florence during restoration work in 1975

13

worried about his own safety because of his close connection to the Medici family. He left Florence just before an angry public drove Piero and the Medici family from the city.

Michelangelo traveled to Bologna, where he stayed for several years. While there, he was commissioned, or hired, to create two marble figures—*St. Petronius* and *Kneeling Angel*—for the tomb of St. Dominic. After he finished, another sculptor accused Michelangelo of stealing his commission. In an effort to keep the peace, Michelangelo left the city and returned to Florence.

Once resettled in Florence, Michelangelo went to work on a marble statue of Eros, the Greek god of love. An imposter art dealer saw the work and told Michelangelo that if the statue looked ancient, he could demand a large sum for it. Michelangelo took the advice,

Bacchus was Michelangelo's first large-scale sculpture and shows the artist's interest in textures, such as those of the skin, hair, and grapes

buried the statue in the ground to make it look old, and shipped it off to Rome, where a cardinal bought it for 200 ducats (about $10,000 in today's money). After he received only 30 ducats, however, Michelangelo angrily set off for Rome and reclaimed the statue.

While in Rome, an Italian gentleman named Jacopo Galli hired Michelangelo to create a 9.5-foot-tall (2.9 m) statue of Bacchus, the Greek god of wine. The statue, completed the next year, portrays the god holding a cup of wine in one hand and a tiger skin and satyr (a woodland deity that is half man, half goat) in the other. Around his head is a garland of vine leaves. A Catholic Church official, Cardinal Rovano, saw the work and thought it showed remarkable talent, so he hired Michelangelo to create a pietá as soon as possible.

Michelangelo was 24 years old when he finished his *Pietá*, a work considered his

first true masterpiece. Observers were astonished at how lifelike the sculpture looked. Not only do the bodies appear to be truly human, but Mary's dress seems to fold like real cloth. Soon after the masterpiece was completed, a sculptor from Milan tried to take credit for the work. To undermine the fraudulent claim, Michelangelo returned to the sculpture one dark night and carved his name along the sash across Mary's chest, making *Pietá* the only known sculpture signed by the artist.

People from all over Italy flocked to Rome to see the spectacular work. Many commented that the Madonna looked younger than the son who lay across her lap. Michelangelo was unfazed by the criticism, simply replying that chaste women stay much fresher than those who are not. The work brought Michelangelo tremendous fame as a master sculptor, and he was suddenly sought out by the most powerful men of the time.

"Through it [*Pietá*], . . . he not only surpassed any other man of his time, and of the time before him, but he even rivaled the ancients."

— *Ascanio Condivi, on Michelangelo's talent as a sculptor*

In 1501, when he was 26 years old, Michelangelo returned to Florence to create his next masterpiece. City officials had a huge block of marble they wanted made into a magnificent work. The block, known as "the Giant," had been abandoned behind a cathedral by a sculptor more than three decades before. Michelangelo had a vision for the marble, and the city officials—impressed with his idea—quickly commissioned him the project and ordered a shed built so Michelangelo could work on the marble in private. In September, the first chisel marks were struck into the block that nearly three years later would become known as the *David*.

Michelangelo's 17-foot (5.2 m) statue is exceptionally beautiful and lifelike. The *David* stands gracefully with one leg slightly bent, a look of worry about his eyes and

brow. The statue revealed to the world Michelangelo's unique artistic vision. Previous sculptures had usually portrayed David after the young warrior's biblical fight with the giant Goliath. Michelangelo's *David*, however, shows David in the moments before the battle was to begin, the sling in his hand. The sculpture is not as perfect as *Pietá*—on *David*'s back are several chisel marks left by the sculptor who originally worked on the block. Yet despite these minor imperfections, the statue earned Michelangelo renown as the greatest sculptor in all of Italy.

From the moment the *David* was unveiled, Michelangelo was overwhelmed with work. The determined and largely antisocial young man spent little time with friends and

Michelangelo's David, which became the symbol of Florence, reveals his careful study of anatomy in its accurate depiction of muscle tension

ABBOZZATO DA MICHELANGIOLO

made no effort to pursue female companionship, instead throwing himself into his art. His next project involved making 12 statues of Jesus Christ's apostles for a cathedral, which were to be completed at the rate of one per year. The artist would begin only the statue of Matthew, however, as he had agreed to several other projects at the same time. One of these jobs entailed painting a mural on the wall of a Florentine council chamber. The project drew crowds from all over the country because another famous Renaissance artist, Leonardo da Vinci, was to paint another wall in the same room at the same time. Neither of the artists finished his work, however—Leonardo because he tried a new technique that didn't work; Michelangelo because he was summoned to Rome by Pope Julius II.

"But in contradiction to so great a genius his nature was so rough and uncouth that his domestic habits were incredibly squalid, and deprived posterity of any pupils who might have succeeded him. Even though he was besought by princes he would never undertake to teach anyone or even allow them to stand watching him work."

— *Paolo Giovio, Bishop of Nocera, on Michelangelo's disagreeable nature*

Pope Julius wanted Michelangelo to create a great tomb of marble in which he would one day be interred. The tomb was to rise 36 feet (11 m) high and be filled with at least 40 statues the size of the *David*. Michelangelo was delighted to be handpicked for such a monumental project and began work on the tomb immediately, completely ignoring his other projects and his few friends in Florence. Unfortunately, his excitement would soon deteriorate in the face of a quarrelsome relationship with one of Europe's most powerful figures.

Michelangelo wanted only the best materials for the tomb and spent the next eight months in Carrara, Italy, supervising the cutting and purchasing of marble. When he ran out of money from Julius, he used his own to pay for additional expenses. Julius, however, learned that it was considered bad luck to build a tomb while one was still alive and immediately stopped all work. Once work halted, Michelangelo went to Rome to obtain reimbursement for his expenses but was turned away several times by the pope. At

last, the frustrated artist left the pope a curtly worded note and departed for Florence. Julius was enraged by Michelangelo's message and sent soldiers after him, but by then the artist was safely inside Florentine territory and could not be arrested. After receiving threats from Julius for seven months, Florentine officials finally asked Michelangelo to leave.

Michelangelo reluctantly returned to Rome and apologized to the pope, who quickly forgave him so he could put the brilliant artist back to work. The dangerous spat behind him, Michelangelo first used bronze—a medium with which he hated to work—to create a giant statue of Julius. As soon as he finished, Julius put him on another project. It was a job Michelangelo didn't want, but it would result in one of the most stunning works the world had ever seen.

Pope Julius disliked the ceiling in Rome's Sistine Chapel. He wanted to transform the drab blue surface decorated with gold stars into something much grander. Since Michelangelo was already at his disposal, Julius ordered the world's greatest living artist to create a masterpiece on the chapel's ceiling.

Michelangelo found the task unappealing for several reasons. He had little experience in fresco painting and feared that the finished product might not turn out as he intended. The job also promised to be time-consuming and very uncomfortable, since the ceiling was nearly 60 feet (18.3 m) high and covered more than 5,400 square feet (500 sq m)—

an area larger than a modern basketball court. Michelangelo at first flatly refused to do the work, but Pope Julius asserted his power and made clear that the task was not an offer but an order.

Michelangelo spent six months preparing for the painting by drawing up plans and making clay figures for study. He hired several assistants when the work began but soon fired them all because they could not live up to his standards of perfection. (What little work they did can still be seen in the ceiling's panels of Noah's life.) Michelangelo ended up painting the remainder of the ceiling alone, using assistants only for menial tasks around the job site.

Michelangelo (left) and Pope Julius II (right) had a stormy relationship, yet Julius was "very well satisfied" with the Sistine Chapel ceiling

27

Soon after the artist commenced painting, a section of the ceiling became badly affected by mold. Seeing the problem as an opportunity to escape the project, Michelangelo approached Julius and said, "I told your Holiness that this was not my [preferred kind of] art; what I have done is spoiled." Julius responded by sending an official to inspect the ceiling. The inspector determined that Michelangelo was applying plaster that was too wet, which encouraged the growth of mold. Informed of this, the pope commanded Michelangelo to fix the problem and continue working. Realizing he would be hard-pressed to find further excuses, Michelangelo resigned himself to completing the painting.

Julius was so impatient to have the ceiling finished that he often came to the chapel to check on Michelangelo's progress. The pope frequently climbed up the scaffolding to get a better look, requiring Michelangelo to put his brushes down and help Julius up onto his platform. Michelangelo grew so frustrated with the pestering that once, when asked when he would have the project finished, he testily snapped, "When I can," a response that so enraged Julius that he threatened to have Michelangelo thrown down from his platform.

Michelangelo devoted four years to the chapel's ceiling, painting it while standing on scaffolding (not lying down as is commonly believed), looking up for most of the day. He ate little during the project and was so exhausted by day's end that he often slept in his dirty clothes at night, paint still splattered on his face. Needing money for both him-

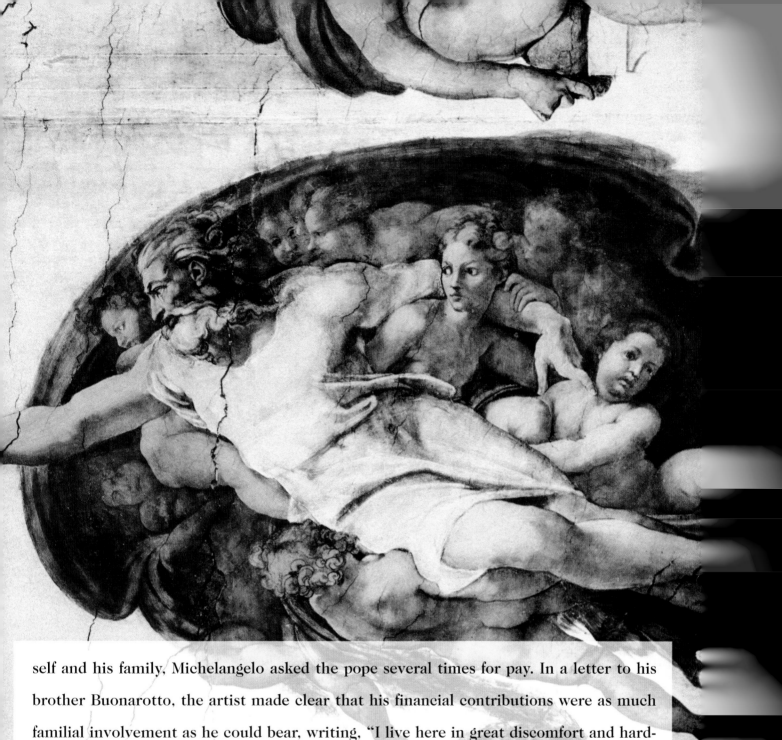

self and his family, Michelangelo asked the pope several times for pay. In a letter to his brother Buonarotto, the artist made clear that his financial contributions were as much familial involvement as he could bear, writing, "I live here in great discomfort and hardship and I have no friends, nor do I want any; and I do not even have time to eat. So I have no wish to be burdened with still more problems [from home], for I could not bear another ounce." For all the work Michelangelo did on the chapel's ceiling, he received 3,000 ducats (an amount equivalent to about $150,000 today).

On October 11, 1512, the finished Sistine Chapel ceiling was revealed to the public. What the throngs of clergymen, officials, and common people saw left them awestruck. In nine panels, biblical stories from the book of Genesis are breathtakingly portrayed in

vibrant colors, and on the edges of the ceiling are painted portraits of Old Testament prophets such as Jonah, Solomon, and David. Half of the ceiling features figures are painted smaller than those on the other side. This happened because after Michelangelo painted the first couple of panels, he studied his work and decided to paint the remainder with larger figures that would be seen more easily. As was the case with his previous works, however, the public didn't really notice this slight imperfection. Such a minor inconsistency did nothing to diminish the splendor of Michelangelo's reluctant masterpiece.

"Every day the work moved him to greater enthusiasm, and he was so spurred on by his own progress that he felt no fatigue and ignored all the discomfort. . . ."

— *Giorgio Vasari, on Michelangelo's work on the Sistine Chapel ceiling*

Pope Julius died in early 1513. Michelangelo planned to work on his tomb, but the next pope—Leo X—summoned the 38-year-old artist for a different job. Leo was Lorenzo de Medici's son Giovanni, and he wanted his old childhood comrade to decorate the front of the family church in San Lorenzo. After three years of delays, the job was suddenly canceled. Leo then asked Michelangelo to build the Medici Chapel and a library in Rome instead. Unfortunately, the pope would never see the buildings' magnificent completion two decades later; he died just as Michelangelo began work on the chapel.

Two more popes were seated and died over the next six years, and Spain's King Charles V attacked Rome in 1527. In a religious frenzy, Protestant soldiers burned and looted the city's churches and murdered Catholic priests and nuns. The beautiful Sistine Chapel was turned into a stable for the soldiers' horses. Fearing for his safety, Michelangelo left for Florence, where he would live in relative seclusion for the next 15 years.

In 1536, at the age of 61, Michelangelo began a project in Rome ordered by Pope Paul III. He was to fill the entire back wall of the Sistine chapel with a scene of the Last Judgment. Michelangelo spent five years painting the scene, portraying Christ high above the chapel's altar and surrounded by angels and saints. Below Christ are demons and sinners in hell, depicted in a chilling and gruesome manner. Michelangelo portrayed himself

Last Judgment was the largest single fresco of the Renaissance and soon became one of the most talked about and copied works of its day

as the sagging skin held by Saint Bartholomew, no doubt a reference to all of the exhausting work piled on him by the various popes.

When *Last Judgment* was revealed in late 1541, it generated mixed reactions. Some people found it terrifying, while others complained about all of the naked bodies in the painting. One papal official was particularly vocal about the nudeness. Reinforcing his notoriously short-tempered and antisocial reputation, Michelangelo responded by painting the official's likeness in the hell portion of the fresco (he is the figure in the bottom left section entwined with a snake and sprouting donkey ears). Two years later, to quell

continued complaints, another artist was hired to paint sections of cloth and draperies over the naked areas of the painting.

After finishing *Last Judgment*, Michelangelo spent the next few years completing Julius's tomb. It was a smaller-scale version of the original plan, with only three of the sculptures coming from Michelangelo. It had taken 40 years, but Michelangelo was finally free of his obligation to Julius. Age and years of strenuous work had made it difficult for the artist to sculpt, and he now spent much more time writing poetry and painting than he did setting chisel to marble.

In 1547, when Michelangelo was 72 years old, Pope Paul III appointed him head architect of Rome's Saint Peter's Basilica. The appointment was an immense honor because the church was to be one of the most important structures in the world, built over the tomb of Saint Peter. Michelangelo accepted the work and refused to take any money for it, considering it his duty to God.

Saint Peter's Basilica would be Michelangelo's last project. At the age of 82, he realized he would not live to see it completed and created a miniature model from which future builders could take their direction. Michelangelo rode a horse to the site every day to supervise the progress. People from all over Italy learned of his routine and visited the city, hoping to catch a glimpse of the legendary artist as he watched the builders work.

"For thirty years now I have wanted to have Michelangelo work for me, and now that I am pope, should I not have my wish?"

— *Pope Paul III*

In the following years, as Michelangelo's health deteriorated, he went through all of his sketches, drawings, and poems and burned what he didn't want others to see, a move that kept secret his creative process. He spent less time in his studio but was there on occasion, working on another pietá that would never be completed. On February 18, 1564, at the age of 89, Michelangelo died. He was buried several days later at Santa Croce Church in Florence. Michelangelo left behind few friends and no family of his own, but he did leave an artistic legacy that will live forever. "I already have a wife who is too much for me; one who keeps me unceasingly struggling on," Michelangelo was heard to say a few years before his death. "It is my art, and my works are my children."

Michelangelo was not only a prolific sculptor and painter, but a writer of numerous letters and poems as well, some of which still exist. He was notoriously difficult to work with, but he also had a witty sense of humor, as seen in the first several verses of the poem below. The poem was written to an unknown recipient and was accompanied by a sketch of a painter in the uncomfortable pose Michelangelo assumed every day. In it, Michelangelo expresses his frustration with the work on the Sistine Chapel ceiling.

I've got myself a goitre from the strain
As water gives the cats in Lombardy,
Or maybe it's in some other country.
My stomach's pushed by force beneath my chin,
My beard towards Heaven, and my brain I feel
Is shoved upon my nape, and my breast is like a Harpy,
And the brush, ever over my face
Makes a rich pavement with its droppings.
My loins have penetrated to my paunch
And as a counterpoise my bottom is a crupper,
And with unseeing eyes my steps I take.
In front of me my skin is stretched
And to bend it, folds itself behind
And stretches like a Syrian bow.
Thus, wrongheaded and strange
Emerge the judgments that the mind brings forth,
In that no good shot comes from a crooked gun.
My painting, when I'm dead, defend it Giovanni,
And my honour too, since I am not in a good place,
And am not a painter either.

The following letter was written by Michelangelo on May 2, 1517, to Domenico Buoninsegni, an official of Pope Leo X. The letter explains the numerous delays and frustrations Michelangelo endured while working on the San Lorenzo church facade before the project was canceled.

Messer Domenico.—Since I last wrote to you, I have not been able to get on with making the model, as I said I would: it would take too long to explain why. I had earlier roughed out something very small, in clay, to make use of here, and although it's puckered like a prune I will send it to you definitely so that you don't think it all a mare's nest.

I've something more to say: and read on patiently for a moment, because it's important. I tell you that I have the will to carry out the construction of the façade of San Lorenzo, so that both in architecture and sculpture it can be the masterpiece for all Italy; but both the Pope and the Cardinal must decide quickly if they want me to do it or not. And if they do want me to do it, they must come to some decision, namely whether to draw up a contract for it with me, and to trust me entirely in everything, or to deal with me in some other way as they think fit, I don't know what. And you will understand why.

As I said I would when I wrote to you, I have ordered many blocks of marble and handed out money here and there, and had the quarrying started in various places. And in some places where I have spent money, the marble produced has not been to my purpose, because of the faults, especially in those large blocks which I need and which I want to have as fine as can be. And in one block that I have already cut, several flaws have shown up near the base whose presence could not be guessed. So two columns I wanted to make from it have not succeeded and I've wasted half my investment on it.

Because of these upsets I've been able to produce so little from so much marble that it will add up to only a few hundred ducats; and so I do not know how to get the accounts to balance, and in the end I won't be able to show I've spent out other than for the marble I shall deliver. I would gladly do like doctor Pier Fantini, but I don't have enough ointment. Also as I am an old man, I don't feel like losing so much time to save the Pope two or three hundred ducats over this marble; and as I am being pressed to get work started, I must therefore have a decision no matter what.

And my decision is this. If I knew I was to have the work and knew the cost, I shouldn't worry about wasting 400 ducats, because I would not have to account for them, and I would snatch three or four of the best men going and commission all the marble from them. And its quality would have to be the same as what I have quarried so far, which is splendid though there is not much of it.

For this and for the money I'd advance them, I would arrange for insurance in Lucca, and I would have the blocks I already possess shipped to Florence and start work on both the Pope's account and my own. But if the Pope's decision isn't made on these lines, I can do nothing; I could not, even if I wished, ship the marble for my work to Florence and then have it shipped back to Rome, but would have to go to Rome to start work as soon as possible because, as I said, I am being pressed.

The cost of the façade, as I intend to design it and have it constructed, including everything, so that afterwards the Pope would not have to bother himself at all, could not, according to the estimate I have made, be less than 35,000 gold ducats. And for this I shall undertake to do it in six years: on the understanding that within 6 months, in respect of the marble, I must needs have at least another 1,000 ducats. And if it does not please the Pope to do this, it will be necessary either that the expenses I have started to incur here for the construction mentioned above go towards my profit or loss, and I must restore the 1,000 ducats to the Pope, or that he obtains someone else to continue with the enterprise, because for several reasons I want to get away from here at all costs.

As for the said price after the work has been started, if at any time it can be done for less, I will approach the Pope and the Cardinal in such good faith that I'll tell them about it far sooner than I would if I were going to be out of pocket myself; but my intention is to do the work in a style which the price may not cover.

Messer Domenico, I beg you to tell me forthwith what's in the mind of the Pope and the Cardinal, and this will please me greatly on top of everything else from you.

[unsigned]

The following letter was written by Michelangelo to either Bishop Marco Vigerio of Sinigaglia or Cardinal Alessandro Farnese regarding the ongoing work on Julius's tomb. The letter was written in October or November 1542 and clearly documents the artist's foul mood over the drawn-out project.

Monsignor.—Your Lordship sends me word that I should paint and not worry about anything else. I reply that one paints with the head and not with the hands; and if he can't keep a clear head a man is lost. So until this business of the tomb is settled, I shan't do any good work. I have not had the ratification of the last contract; and on the strength of the other contract, drawn up in Pope Clement's presence, people stone me every day just as if I had crucified Christ.

I say that to my knowledge the contract was not read over in the presence of Pope Clement as the copy I received later said it was. What happened was that Clement sent me to Florence the same day, and then the ambassador Gianmaria da Modena who was with the notary had him add to it in the way he wanted. Through this, when I returned and inspected it, I found that it specified 1,000 ducats more than had been fixed for me to pay; that the house I live in was included in the contract; and there were several other traps to destroy me, which Pope Clement would never have allowed. And Fra Sebastiano can bear witness that he wished me to let the Pope know all this and to have the notary hanged. I would not do this, because I was not bound to do anything I could not have done had things been left as they were. I swear that I know nothing of having had the money the contract mentions and as alleged by Gianmaria. But let us agree that I did have the money since I've acknowledged receipt, and I cannot withdraw from the contract; and let's add more money besides, if more is claimed; and heap it all together. And then look at what I've done for Pope Julius at Bologna, Florence, and at Rome, in bronze, marble, and painting, and all the time I stayed with him, which was as long as he was Pope; and judge what I deserve. I say in good conscience, with reference to the salary that Pope Paul gives me, that I am owed 5,000 crowns by the heirs of Pope Julius.

I also say this: that the reward from Pope Julius for my labours having been what it was (my fault for not knowing how to manage my affairs) were it not for what Pope Paul has given me, I would today be dying of hunger. Yet according to those ambassadors, I must have enriched myself and stolen from the altar. They make a great song and dance, and I know I should shut them up, but I haven't the strength.

Gianmaria, who was ambassador at the time of the old Duke, in Clement's presence, after the contract was made and I had returned from Florence and was starting to work on Julius's tomb, said to me that if I wanted to do the Duke a great favour, I should clear off altogether for he didn't care about the tombs but he couldn't stand the idea of my working for Pope Paul. Then I realized why he had brought my house into the contract: to get shot of me and grab possession on the authority of that document; it's clear enough what tricks they're up to, and they are bringing shame on our enemies and their own masters.

The fellow who came to see me just now wanted to know all about what I had in Florence; that was his first question, before he asked to see what stage the work for the tomb had reached. And so I find that I have lost all my youth tied to this tomb, defending it as best I could against the demands of Pope Leo and Clement. And my too trusting nature has gone unrewarded and been my ruin. That was my bad fortune! I see many who lie in bed and enjoy incomes of 2,000 or 3,000 crowns, while I wear myself out with my labours only to stay poor.

But to return to painting: I can deny nothing to Pope Paul. And I shall paint miserably and make miserable things. I've written this to your Lordship, so that when it's opportune you will be better able to tell the truth to the Pope; I'll be glad for the Pope to learn the truth and to know what's behind the war waged against me. Let them understand, who can.

Your Lordship's servant, Michelangelo

1475

Michelangelo is born in Caprese, Italy, on March 6.

1488

Michelangelo becomes an apprentice of artist Domenico Ghirlandaio.

1490

Michelangelo moves into the Medici palace in Florence and studies the art of sculpting.

1499

Pietá, Michelangelo's first true masterpiece, is finished in Rome.

1501

Michelangelo returns to Florence and begins work on the David.

1504

The completion of the David *establishes Michelangelo as the greatest sculptor in Italy.*

1505

Pope Julius II commissions Michelangelo to create his tomb.

1506

Pope Julius II halts all work on the tomb; Michelangelo's attempts to obtain reimbursement for his expenses cause a rift with the pope.

1508

Pope Julius II has Michelangelo begin painting the ceiling of the Sistine Chapel.

1512

The Sistine Chapel ceiling is completed and revealed to the public in October.

1513

Pope Julius II dies; Michelangelo begins working for Pope Leo X.

1520

Michelangelo's work on the Medici family church in San Lorenzo is suddenly canceled.

1527

Rome is attacked by the army of Spanish king Charles V; Michelangelo flees to Florence.

1536

Michelangelo begins working on Last Judgment *in Rome.*

1541

Michelangelo completes Last Judgment; *it is unveiled to the public in October.*

1545

Michelangelo finishes the tomb of Pope Julius II after 40 years of sporadic work.

1547

Michelangelo is appointed head architect of Saint Peter's Basilica in Rome by Pope Paul III.

1564

Michelangelo dies in Rome at the age of 89.

Angelo Poliziano — *A renowned Italian poet and scholar; he taught classic works of literature to Michelangelo and the sons of Florentine ruler Lorenzo de Medici*

Bertoldo di Giovanni — *An Italian sculptor and assistant to the painter Donatello; he is believed to have taught Michelangelo to sculpt while employed by Lorenzo de Medici*

Domenico Ghirlandaio — *A famous and popular Italian fresco painter who painted some of the walls of the Sistine Chapel and ran a successful art workshop in Florence*

ducat — *A gold coin used as currency in 16th-century Rome; one ducat was the equivalent of about $50 in today's money*

fresco — *An art technique in which paint is applied to wet plaster, and once it dries, the coloring remains vibrant for a long time; the word* fresco *is Italian for "fresh"*

Julius II — *A pope who was one of the greatest papal art patrons of the Renaissance period; he was also known as the "Warrior Pope," as he was involved in many military efforts*

Leo X — *A pope whose extravagant lifestyle both depleted the papal treasury and helped make the papacy a more prominent power; he was the second son of Lorenzo de Medici*

Marsilio Ficino — *A famous Renaissance physician and philosopher renowned for his interpretations of the ideas of the Greek philosopher Plato*

Medici — *A wealthy and powerful family that in effect ruled Florence for much of the Renaissance; the family rose to prominence as bankers and were great art patrons*

pietá — *A religious theme or representation in which the Virgin Mary is shown supporting the body of the dead Christ; the word* pietá *is Italian for "piety"*

podesta — *An Italian government official of the Middle Ages who was appointed to govern a city for six months or a year; the word* podesta *is Italian for "power"*

Renaissance — *A period of renewed interest in arts and sciences that began in Italy and Northern Europe around 1400 and lasted until about 1600*

Sistine Chapel — *The main church structure of the Catholic Church; it was built in Rome between 1475 and 1483*